Birds

A Compare and Contrast Book
by Aszya Summers

There are more than 10,000 different species of birds in the world, and over 900 in North America alone! From birds of prey to shorebirds to backyard songbirds, birds are some of the most varied and abundant animals on earth.

What do birds have in common and how are they different?

American Dipper

American Flamingo

Common Raven

Northern Flicker

Piping Plover

Northern Cardinal

Red-tailed Hawk

Barn Swallow

Mallard

White-tailed Ptarmigan

The easiest way to tell a bird from other animals is that birds are always covered in feathers. In fact, they are the only animals that have feathers!

Feathers can look very different on different birds!

Owls, like this Barn Owl, have special feathers that let them fly silently to sneak up on their prey. The feather "dishes" around owl eyes help them collect sounds to find prey.

Atlantic Puffins waterproof their feathers for life in the open ocean and diving to catch fish.

Peregrine Falcons use dark feathers under their eyes, like face paint used by football players, to reduce glare and catch prey in midair.

Other birds, like the Scissor-tailed Flycatcher, use their long tail feathers to impress mates with fancy dances in the air.

Tufted Titmouses have a crest of feathers on top of their heads. They can raise or lower the feathers to attract a mate or to communicate with other birds.

Many male birds have bright feather colors to help them attract a mate. The bright colors also draw attention away from nests if animals or humans approach.

Females are not as bright and colorful to better camouflage when sitting on nests.

Can you tell which are males or females?

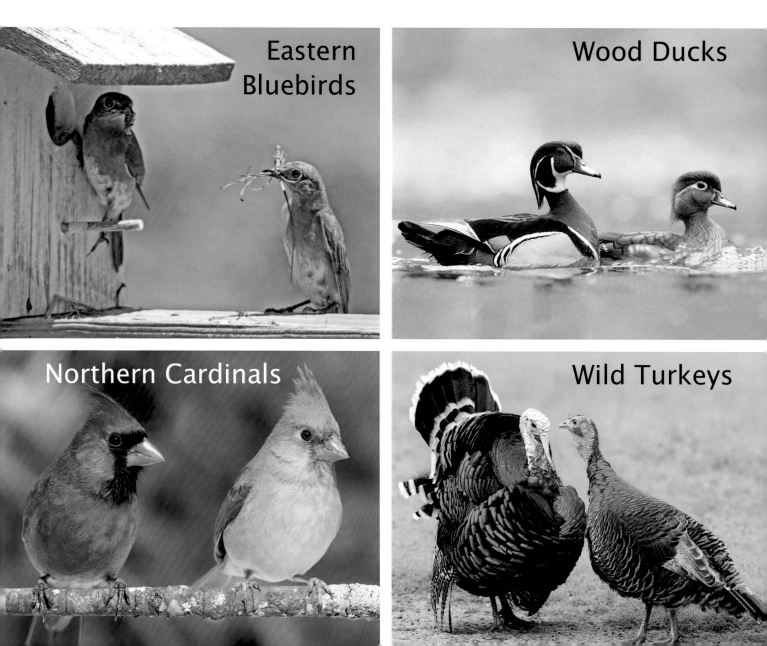

Eastern Bluebirds

Wood Ducks

Northern Cardinals

Wild Turkeys

Ring-necked Pheasants

Rose-breasted Grosbeaks

American Goldfinches

Painted Buntings

Ruby-throated Hummingbirds

House Finches

Birds come in all different sizes.

Some birds are very tall. Whooping Cranes are the tallest bird in North America. They can be over five feet (1.5 m) tall!

How tall are you?

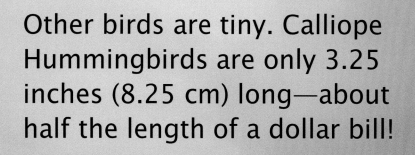

Other birds are tiny. Calliope Hummingbirds are only 3.25 inches (8.25 cm) long—about half the length of a dollar bill!

Birds don't have teeth, they have beaks. Every bird has a unique beak to help it eat exactly what it needs.

House Finches have short, thick beaks that are perfect for eating their favorite foods—seeds!

Red-bellied Woodpeckers have long, strong beaks to drill holes in trees looking for insects.

Roseate Spoonbills use their spoon-like beaks as nets to scoop up tiny animals and plants in the water.

Bald Eagles use their sharp, curved beaks to tear prey into small pieces to eat.

Brown Pelicans have a pouch attached to their beaks. When they capture fish, they release the water and then swallow the fish whole!

Bird's legs and feet are used in a lot of different ways to help them live in their different habitats!

Sometimes we can learn about a bird based on what their legs and feet look like! For example, we can infer that birds with webbed feet swim. Birds with sharp talons or claws to grab prey are meat eaters.

Wading birds, like this Greater Yellowlegs, have super long legs for wading through shallow water to search for food. Their toes spread to keep them from sinking into the loose mud.

Swimming birds, like this Atlantic Puffin, have strong, webbed feet to swim and dive deep into the water to catch fish.

Birds of prey, like this Osprey, have sharp claws or talons to grab and carry their prey.

Some birds, like this Carolina Wren, have three toes pointing forward and one pointing backward. They wrap their toes around branches to hold on.

Climbing birds, like this Pileated Woodpecker, have four sharp, curved claws to hold onto tree bark. Two toes point forward, and two point backwards.

All birds lay eggs.

Many birds that lay their eggs on the ground, like this Killdeer, have speckled eggs to help camouflage their eggs.

Other birds, like the American Robin, lay beautiful, colorful eggs. Some scientists think these colors may help the eggs stay the perfect temperature while the babies grow inside.

Birds have many different ways to build nests.

Ospreys build huge nests out of sticks and other plant materials. They use the same nest every year. Some nests can get as big as ten feet (three meters) tall!

Cliff Swallows use mud, lined with feathers and soft plants. They often nest in huge colonies, sometimes with thousands of nests in a single location!

Barn Swallows build nests out of mud, grass, and feathers in chimneys and around the eves of houses.

Loons build nests out of twigs, grasses, reeds, and other aquatic vegetation near water.

Orioles weave long grasses, feathers, or even strings they might find into long, hanging nests. Those strings can be dangerous to the birds.

Osprey

Cliff Swallow

Common Loon

Baltimore Oriole

Barn Swallow

When baby birds first hatch, they need lots of help from their parents to grow up.

Many bird parents work together to catch food and feed chicks until they are ready to fly. That can take several weeks.

Anna's Hummingbirds

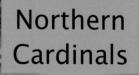

Northern Cardinals

Eastern Bluebirds

Red-winged Blackbird

With the exception of a few species, birds have hollow bones allowing them to save energy as they fly through the air.

Some birds, like Great Cormorants, are more suited for "flying" though the water than through air!

While Lesser Roadrunners found in the Southwestern U.S. can fly, they prefer to run.

However they move, it's important for birds to be able to get food and escape predators.

Canada Geese

Great Cormorant

Lesser Roadrunner

Strong wings are important for some birds to get liftoff, especially for heavier birds. At 20 pounds (9 kg), California Condors are the heaviest bird in North America. To help them fly, their wingspan is a massive 10 feet (3 m). They often jump off of cliffs so they don't have to work so hard to fly!

Other birds, like Chimney Swifts, have short, pointed wings. These wings help these airborne acrobats catch tiny insects in midair.

Changing seasons affect birds. In areas where it gets too cold for them or for their food in the winter, many birds fly to warmer areas or migrate. You might even see birds migrating in the spring or fall.

Arctic Terns are champion migrants. They fly 25,000 miles (over 40,000 km) each year, from the north pole all the way to the south pole!

Wild Turkeys have lots of thick, warm feathers. By eating a wide variety of foods, they stay in cold-weather climates year-round! Turkeys also carry lots of extra fat, and usually prefer running to flying to get around!

Covered in feathers, flying through the air, hollow bones, nests, and so much more! Birds are busy thriving in different kinds of habitats all across North America, in every place you can imagine.

If you were a bird, what kind of adaptations would you have? Where would you live?

Black-billed Magpies

Sandhill Cranes

Common Loon

Short-eared Owl

Black-capped Chickadee

Great Blue Heron

Brown-crested
Flycatcher

Royal
Terns

American Oystercatcher

Gambel's Quail

For Creative Minds

Beginning Birders

If you are interested in looking for wildlife, birds are the perfect place to start! Looking for birds outside is a great way to learn that nature isn't just in parks or special, protected places. You can find birds anywhere and everywhere.

Tips for finding birds: Use all your senses to find birds in your neighborhood. Scan anywhere that might make a good home for a bird with your eyes. Maybe there's one napping up in the trees, or in a shady place behind your house. Use your ears too. Birds sing all the time! Quite often, you will hear a bird before you ever see it. Once you hear a bird, close your eyes and see if you can figure out where the song is coming from.

Follow the signs: Birds leave signs that they have been hanging around. Check branches for pieces of nests. In the spring, you may get lucky enough to find a whole bird nest or egg pieces! Check tree trunks, especially dead trees, for woodpecker holes. And keep an eye out for tracks, feathers, or poop.

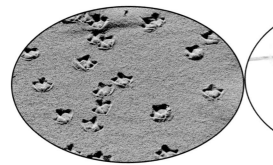

tracks in sand, mud, or snow feather bird poop

Bring them to you: You can make many easy, homemade bird feeders. Coating a pinecone with peanut butter or honey, and then rolling it in sunflower seeds is a great way to bring everything from goldfinches to cardinals right to your window!

Observe your new friends: Build your science skills by watching your new bird friends and writing or drawing what you see. It can be fun to watch what different kinds of birds live in what habitats, or are seen more often in what weather. Use all these tips to become a birding expert!

Not Just for the Birds!

Life as a bird is very different from ours in a lot of ways, but in some ways it is very similar! Think about each thing that a bird can do below. Describe what tools you use to do some of the things birds do.

To move from one place to another, most birds spread their wings and fly. *How can you fly from place to place?*

When it gets cold, birds tuck in their legs and fluff up their feathers to keep warm. *What can you use when it gets too cold?*

Hummingbirds use a long, thin, hollow beak to slurp liquid nectar out of flowers. *What can you use to drink liquid out of a container?*

Many meat-eating birds use their sharp beaks to slice meat into smaller pieces that fit into their mouth. *What do you use to cut food into smaller pieces?*

Pelicans use their huge beak to scoop up a mouthful of water and fish, and then drain out the water to keep just the fish! *Is there a tool you can use to scoop solid objects, like fish, out of a liquid?*

Woodpeckers use a strong, sharp beak to peck holes in trees to find bugs. *What tool would we use to make holes in wood?*

Whose Foot?

With so many birds in so many different places, many of them have lots of different adaptations to help them survive in their habitat. Take a close look at each foot and match it to the bird in its habitat! Think about what each foot might be helpful for.

Answers: 1D-Mallards use webbed feet to paddle and swim through the water. 2A-Ospreys use strong, sharp talons to catch fish. 3B-Stellar's Jays use their feet to grip onto small branches in the trees. 4C-Northern Bobwhites have strong, flat feet as they spend most of their days walking through tall grass searching for seeds.

Conservation Connections

Some of the most creative conservation solutions have come from the conservation of North American birds. Conservationists, or people who work to protect species from extinction, work every day to protect endangered species across North America. Conservation work requires dedication, hard work, and a lot of creativity.

California Condors nest on cliffs or mountaintops along the Pacific coast. Threatened by habitat loss, hunting and egg collecting, there were only 22 birds left in the wild by 1987. The birds were captured and taken to zoos for breeding. Caretakers raised the chicks using puppets and costumes to teach them all the skills they would need to survive when released back in the wild. There are now over 400 condors in the wild and the zoo-breeding program is still being used.

By the 1940s, the number of Whooping Cranes had dropped from thousands to one flock of less than 30. Female cranes usually lay two eggs a season, but normally only one survives. Scientists gathered the second eggs and raised the chicks using costumes. To protect the cranes from a flood or other disaster, they wanted a second flock of cranes. Conservationists taught the birds a new migration route using an ultralight aircraft by a person in a crane costume. Today, there are hundreds of cranes living back in the wild.

One of the biggest threats to the Bald Eagle was pesticides like DDT. When it was discovered that the chemicals caused eagle eggshells to become too thin to protect the unborn chicks, there were less than 500 breeding pairs of bald eagles in the U.S. After years of research and pushing for more careful use of pesticides, DDT was banned and Bald Eagles began to recover. In 2007, the Bald Eagle was taken off the endangered species list, and today is once again a common sight across North America.

To Mom, Dad, and Jess, for 30 years of tolerating my interruptions pointing out every animal everywhere—AS

A note from the editor: This book uses the names and capitalization recommended by the North American Classification and Nomenclature Committee of the American Ornithological Society.

Thanks to Christina Lavallee, Lead Keeper, Animal Ambassadors at Zoo Atlanta for verifying the information in this book.

All photographs are licensed through Adobe Stock Photos or Shutterstock.

Library of Congress Cataloging-in-Publication Data

Names: Summers, Aszya, 1992- author.
Title: Birds : a compare and contrast book / Aszya Summers.
Description: Mt. Pleasant, SC : Arbordale Publishng, LLC, [2023] | Includes
   bibliographical references.
Identifiers: LCCN 2022036984 (print) | LCCN 2022036985 (ebook) | ISBN
   9781643519845 (paperback) | ISBN 9781638170037 (interactive
   dual-language, read along) | ISBN 9781638170419 (epub) | ISBN
   9781638170228 (adobe pdf)
Subjects: LCSH: Birds--Juvenile literature.
Classification: LCC QL676.2 .S86 2023 (print) | LCC QL676.2 (ebook) | DDC
   598--dc23/eng/20220804
LC record available at https://lccn.loc.gov/2022036984
LC ebook record available at https://lccn.loc.gov/2022036985

Translated into Spanish: *Aves: Un libro de comparaciones y contrastes*
Spanish paperback ISBN: 9781638172642
Spanish ePub ISBN: 9781638172826
Spanish PDF ebook ISBN: 9781638172765
Dual-language read-along available online at www.fathomreads.com

English Lexile® Level: 940L

Bibliography

"Audubon Guide to North American Birds." Audubon, 2019, www.audubon.org/bird-guide.
"Backyard Bird Identification Guide (Identify Your Visitors)." Backyardbirdingblog.com, 1 July 2015, backyardbirdingblog.com/backyard-bird-identification-guide/.
"Birds of North America - North American Birds." Birds-of-North-America.net, 2019, www.birds-of-north-america.net/.
Kazilek, CJ. "23 Functions of Feathers". ASU - Ask A Biologist. 30 Sep 2009. ASU - Ask A Biologist, Web. 7 May 2021. https://askabiologist.asu.edu/content/23-functions-feathers
"Online Bird Guide, Bird ID Help, Life History, Bird Sounds from Cornell." All about Birds, 2019, www.allaboutbirds.org.
"Types of Bird Feet." Robinsonlibrary.com, robinsonlibrary.com/science/zoology/birds/general/feet.htm.

Printed in the US
This product conforms to CPSIA 2008

Arbordale Publishing, LLC
Mt. Pleasant, SC 29464
www.ArbordalePublishing.com